Brian Deakin

William and Margaret

Three scenes to read and act

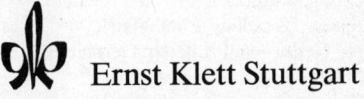
Ernst Klett Stuttgart

Contents

The Case of the Moslem Ladies 3
All Expenses Paid 12
The Case of the Diamond Bracelet 21

1. Auflage 1 ⁴ ³ ² ¹ / 1979 78 77 76

Alle Drucke dieser Auflage können im Unterricht nebeneinander benutzt werden. Die letzte Zahl bezeichnet das Jahr dieses Druckes.
© Ernst Klett Verlag, Stuttgart 1976. Alle Rechte vorbehalten.
Zeichnungen: Richard Kennedy, Maidenhead.
Druck: Gutmann, Heilbronn. Printed in Germany.
ISBN 3-12-571160-6

The Case of the Moslem Ladies

William Martin is an English boy of about fourteen who is staying with his aunt, Margaret Simpson, in London. This morning they have gone to a big department store in Oxford Street, where they are going to buy a birthday present for Margaret's brother, William's Uncle George.

Margaret: Here we are at last.
William: Be careful of your bag in the crowd.
Margaret: Why do you say that?
William: I read in the paper yesterday that in London one person in twenty is a thief.

case Fall

Margaret: I know. Isn't it terrible? Of course it's all these foreigners who come here for holidays. They have to make money *somehow* to pay their hotel bills.

William: People should help the police more. I'm going to be a detective one day. It must be very exciting.

Margaret: Sometimes it's too exciting. But certainly we must all help the police.

William: The Men's Department is over there, if you want to buy a pullover for Uncle George.

Margaret: Oh yes. I see it. It's on the other side of the Food Department. Come on.

They walk towards the Men's Department. William begins to laugh when he sees two women dressed in strange clothes.

William: Look at those two women. They're completely *covered* in white from head to foot, and you can only see their eyes.

Margaret: They're Moslem women, you see. They're not allowed to show their faces. That's why they're wearing *veils*.

William: But look what they're doing now.

Margaret: They're buying biscuits, cheese and a chicken. What's wrong with that? Even foreigners must eat, you know.

William: But they're not paying for anything. The tall one is giving things to the smaller one, and she's putting them under her long dress.

Margaret: So she is! Good heavens, they're *shop-lifting!*

somehow irgendwie
to cover (in) einhüllen
veil [veil] Schleier
shop-lifting Ladendiebstahl

William: There goes a bottle of whisky. No, two.
Margaret: I'm going *to expose* them at once.
William: Don't you think we should find the store detective first?
Margaret: There isn't time. Come on. Be quick.
William: I'll stand behind them so that they can't escape.

They hurry across the Food Department and in a loud voice Margaret tells the girl shop-assistant about the two women. The shop-assistant is not surprised because she has already had two cases of the same thing that morning. She rings an alarm bell and the store detective rushes to the counter. He takes William by one arm and Margaret by another.

Detective: Just come with me, you two. Ring the police, Miss Carter, if you don't mind.
Margaret: What are you doing? Take your hands off me, young man.
William: Those foreign ladies are the ones who are stealing. We are the ones who caught them.
Assistant: He's right. They are the ones who came and told me.
Detective: So you foreigners were stealing, were you? Come with me.

The detective tries to take them away but the taller foreign lady speaks to him in a deep voice and stops him.

Taller lady: You may be interested to know, my man, that *I* am *Princess* Fatima of *Abu Majumba*.

---

to expose s. o. [iksˈpəuz] jdn entlarven
princess Prinzessin
Abu Majumba [ˌæbuːməˈdʒʌmbə] erfundener Ländername

William: Abu Majumba? Isn't that one of the oil-rich countries?
Smaller lady: It certainly is.
Margaret: Haven't you enough money with all that oil? Do you really need to steal?
Detective: Oh, what a terrible mistake! Princess Fatima, of course. We were expecting you ... they telephoned. Oh dear, I'm very sorry. Believe me, it will never happen again.
William: But we saw them with our own eyes. She was taking things and the other one was putting them under her dress.
Detective: Be quiet. You don't understand. They explained on the telephone. The Princess never *handles* money herself. She gives things to her *lady-in-waiting,* who pays later.

to handle anfassen
lady-in-waiting Hofdame

Margaret: Oh, I see. I'm so sorry. We thought ...
Taller lady: And now please ask these awful people to go away so that we can continue our shopping.
Detective: At once, madam. A terrible mistake! If I can help you in any way ...
Taller lady: We don't allow such things in *my* country.
Smaller lady: Off with their heads! Off with their heads!

The two foreign ladies are very angry and walk away to continue their shopping. The detective speaks to William and Margaret in a very cold voice because he is angry, too, and then he leaves them.

Detective: Please be more careful next time you try to do my work for me. You nearly lost us a very important customer then.
Margaret: We were only trying to help. People never thank you for anything these days.
William: Come on, *Auntie*. There are the pullovers.
Margaret: And there's Mrs Marshall. I didn't know she had left the Ladies Dress Department. How are you, Mrs Marshall?
Mrs Marshall: Very well, Miss Simpson, thank you. And you?
Margaret: Quite well, thank you. I'm looking for a pullover for my brother. He's very tall so it must be a large one.
Mrs Marshall: What about this Scottish one? It's very warm.
William: Isn't that lovely? I should like one of those.
Margaret: Well, it isn't *your* birthday. Is it very expensive?
Mrs Marshall: No. It's only £11.
Margaret: Then I'll take it. Put it on my *account*, please.

Off with their heads! Kopf ab!
Auntie [ˈɑːnti] Tantchen
account [əˈkaunt] Konto

7

Mrs Marshall: Of course.
William: Auntie, look who's coming this way.
Margaret: Who?
William: Uncle George.
Margaret: Oh dear! I wanted the present to be a surprise. Quick, William, put the pullover under your raincoat.

She gives the pullover to William and he puts it under his raincoat so that Uncle George won't see it. But the two foreign ladies are still quite near, and they see it and think William is stealing.

George: Hello, you two. Spending too much money again, Margaret?
Margaret: For once I think you're right, George.
George: What are you buying in the Men's Department? Something for William?
William: Unfortunately not. We're...
Taller Moslem lady: They're not buying anything. They're shoplifting.
Smaller lady: Yes, we saw it with our own eyes. That boy put a pullover under his coat.
Taller lady: Ring the alarm bell, Muna.

The smaller lady rushes behind the counter and rings the alarm bell. The detective hurries to them. When he reaches Princess Fatima, he rubs his hands together and *bows* to the ground.

Detective: Oh, Princess Fatima. What can I do for you?
Taller lady: These awful people are shop-lifting. The boy put a pullover under his coat. There it is.

to bow [bau] sich verbeugen

She pulls a bit of the pullover out but William quickly puts it back again.

Detective: So that's your game, is it? You say that other people are shop-lifting and you're doing it yourself. Come with me.
Margaret: Oh no, we can explain. You see ...
Mrs Marshall: They certainly haven't stolen anything. I know Miss Simpson and ...
George: Just a minute. Who did you say this lady was?
Detective: Princess Fatima of Abu Majumba, and that's her lady-in-waiting.
William: They were buying whisky and things, and we thought they were shop-lifting because they weren't paying.
Margaret: They don't understand England. They're Moslem ladies from one of the oil-rich countries.
George: No, they aren't. I've read about these two in the newspapers. They are *neither* Moslems *nor* ladies. Moslems don't drink whisky and ... look here.

He pulls away the taller lady's veil. They now see a man's face with a big, black *moustache*.

Detective: Good heavens!
Taller lady: Come on, Joe. This is no place for us.
Margaret: After them, William!

As the smaller "lady" is called Joe, he is clearly a man, too. Both "ladies" run away and William and Margaret, Uncle George, the detective and Mrs Marshall run after them. After a few minutes

---

neither ... nor ['naiðə] weder ... noch
moustache [məs'tɑːʃ] Schnurrbart

they all meet again near the door of the department store but no one has found the two "ladies". Suddenly William sees them in the Furniture Department and they all run across to the "ladies", who are quietly looking at furniture. The detective puts his arms round the taller one and throws him on to a bed. Uncle George catches the smaller one. Both scream in high voices.

Ladies: Help! Help! They are trying *to kidnap* us. Mustafa! Help! Mohammed! Where are you?

Two *Arab* guards rush in and throw themselves on to the detective and Uncle George. Both ladies continue to scream.

Mrs Marshall: There are more than two of them, then.
William: I'll go and fetch the police.
Margaret: Stop it at once. Those two are not women, they're men. And they were shop-lifting.
Guard: That is not possible. This is Princess Fatima of Abu Majumba.
Princess: And this is my lady-in-waiting. What does this mean? I have never been so *insulted* in my life.
William: The voice is not the same.
Margaret: Oh dear! This must be the real Princess Fatima.
Princess: Of course I'm the *real* Princess Fatima, and I have been insulted. I shall never come near this shop again. We don't allow such things in *my* country.

---

to kidnap entführen
Arab ['ærəb] Araber, arabisch
to insult [in'sʌlt] beleidigen
real echt

Lady-in-waiting: Off with their heads! Off with their heads!
Princess: Mustafa, take us to the car at once.
Detective: Quick. Fetch the manager, somebody. Quickly, before they leave the store. If we lose them, I shall lose my job.
Mrs Marshall: I'll go and fetch him.
Margaret: And we have more shopping to do. Goodbye, everybody.
George: Is there anything more we can do?
Detective: No!! You have done enough already. I'm going to lose my job. Go away!
Margaret: All right, we're going. Come on, George. Do you still want to be a detective one day, William?
William: Perhaps not. But I still want to help the police. After all the first two *were* shop-lifting, weren't they?

Questions

1. What are William and Margaret going to do in Oxford Street?
2. Why does Margaret want to expose the two Moslem women?
3. Who made the "terrible mistake"? William and Margaret or the detective?
4. Why is the detective angry with William and Margaret?
5. Describe the pullover that Margaret buys. How much is it?
6. Why does William put the pullover under his raincoat?
7. What is the detective's second mistake?
8. How do you know that the two "ladies" are not ladies at all?
9. What happens to the real Princess Fatima and her lady-in-waiting?
10. Do you think that the detective is going to lose his job? Why?

All Expenses Paid

It is Wednesday morning. On Friday William and Margaret are going to Paris for a few days. They have gone to a *toy* shop to buy a birthday present for William's cousin, Robert, the son of Uncle George.

Margaret: I must get Robert's present today. We'll be in Paris on his birthday. They're a terrible family, aren't they? Their birthdays all come at the same time.

William: What are you going to buy him this time?

Margaret: I don't know. Presents for children are so difficult.

William: How old is he exactly?

Margaret: He'll be ten on Monday.

William: Buy him a guitar.

Margaret: You only say that because *you* want a guitar. Robert's too young.

Shop-assistant: Can I help you, madam?

Margaret: Yes. I'm looking for a present for a boy of ten.

Shop-assistant: I think we have just the thing. What about this toy *machine-gun?* They're American.

William: It looks very like a real one. Can you fire it?

Shop-assistant: No, you can't exactly fire it. But you don't need to fire it to frighten people. The *sight* of it is enough.

Margaret: It's not a good idea to give guns to children. They become too aggressive.

expenses [iks'pensiz] Unkosten
toy Spielzeug
machine-gun Maschinengewehr
sight Anblick

A small boy comes into the shop with his father, a young man about twenty-five. The boy picks up the gun and points it at Margaret. He shouts: "Ta-ta-ta-ta-ta-ta".

Margaret: You see. No, I think I'll buy some more animals for Robert's toy farm.
Shop-assistant: Very good, madam.
Margaret: You choose them, William.
Boy: Can I have that gun, Dad? Please!
Man: How much is it?
Shop-assistant: £6
Man: Haven't you got a cheaper one?
Shop-assistant: I'm afraid we haven't. And we only have a few of these.

Margaret: I'm glad to hear that. If you're not careful, young man, your son will be a *criminal* one day.
Man: That has nothing to do with you. It's not your business.
Margaret: It's everybody's business when children turn into criminals.
Boy: Let me have the gun, Dad. It's my birthday tomorrow.
William: Auntie, do you think Robert will be a farmer one day because he plays with a farm now?
Margaret: Be quiet, William. That has nothing to do with it.
Man: I want my son to be a man. I'll take that gun.
Boy: Ooh, good!
Margaret: And I'll have five cows, two pigs and a dozen hens.
Man: Pigs and hens! What a present!
Shop-assistant: That will be £ 2.45 p, madam. Pay at the cash desk.
Margaret: Thank you. Come on, William. If parents allow their children to play with dangerous toys, there's nothing we can do about it.

Margaret and William go to the cash desk to pay, and then leave the shop. The aggressive boy points the gun at Margaret again and shouts: "Ta-ta-ta-ta-ta-ta."

The next day William and Margaret go to the bank to get the *traveller's cheques* and French money for their trip. They are talking to the *cashier,* Miss Kennedy.

---

criminal ['krimɪnəl] Verbrecher
That has nothing to do with you. It's not your business. Das geht Sie nichts an.
traveller's cheque Reisescheck
cashier [kæˈʃiə] Kassierer(in)

William: Do you think we'll have enough money?

Margaret: I hope so. We're only staying a few days and I have £50 in traveller's cheques.

Miss Kennedy: And here is £10 in French money, Miss Simpson.

Margaret: Of course. I'd forgotten that. You see, William we'll have plenty.

William: But what shall we do in an emergency? I mean, perhaps you'll be taken to hospital suddenly. Perhaps you'll even be kidnapped.

Miss Kennedy: You *are* a pessimistic young man.

Margaret: Isn't he? But he always thinks terrible things will happen to me, never to himself.

Miss Kennedy: Here are your passports. The money you're taking is written on the last page.

Margaret: Thank you. And now we must hurry. We have to pack.

The door of the bank suddenly opens and two men with *stockings* on their heads enter. One is holding a machine-gun. Another bank *robber,* without a stocking on his head, has driven a taxi to the bank and is waiting for the others outside. The first robber, who has no gun, comes right into the bank to collect the money. The second robber, the one with the gun, stands at the door so that he can look out and see if anyone is coming. He points the gun at the customers and bank clerks.

1st robber: This is a *hold-up*. Keep calm and you will be all right.

stocking Strumpf
robber Räuber
hold-up Überfall

2nd robber: Anyone who goes near the alarm is as good as dead. Quiet! Another word and I'll shoot.

1st robber: Hey, you! Take this *sack* and put the money in it.

William: Who? Me?

1st robber: Yes, you.

William: B-but I d-don't know where the money is.

1st robber: The cashier's got it of course. Jump over the counter. Quick.

Margaret: William, stay where you are.

2nd robber: Shut up, you. You open your mouth too often. Get the money, William, if that's your name.

1st robber: On the floor, everybody. Faces to the ground. Quick now.

sack Sack

Margaret: I am *not* going to lie on the floor. And William, put that sack down and come with me. We are leaving this bank at once. We have to pack.
William: B-b-but he has a g-g-gun.
2nd robber: And I'll use it, too.
Margaret: Never mind the gun. He won't *dare* to shoot me. Come on. What's the matter with you?

Margaret walks towards the door of the bank, her head high, and William follows her. The first robber throws himself on William and pulls him back but William manages to put the sack over the man's head. The second robber does not fire the gun but hits Margaret with it, and she is so angry that she hits him with her umbrella. While the two robbers are busy with William and Margaret someone tries to ring the alarm but it doesn't work. Bank clerks and customers now throw themselves on the two robbers and hold them. The second robber's gun is taken away from him and the police are telephoned. Margaret and William manage to get outside at last.

Margaret: What luck! There's a taxi at the door.
William: But it's taken.
Margaret: Never mind. There's nobody in it and this is an emergency. Open the door.
Taxi man: Hey! This taxi's not free. I'm waiting for someone in the bank.
William: It's an emergency. Some gangsters tried to rob the bank.
Margaret: But they didn't manage it. They were only amateurs. To the police station. Quickly.

to dare ['dɛə] wagen

William: The taxi man's getting out.
Margaret: Where are you going? Come back.
Taxi man: I'm just going to get some cigarettes. I shan't be a minute.
Margaret: Now we won't get to the police station after all.
William: Never mind. Look. The police have arrived already. We can tell them here.

The police rush into the bank, followed by William and Margaret. Five or six people are holding each bank robber. The bank manager hurries to Margaret.

Bank manager: Oh, madam. Thank you so much. You were wonderful. Such *bravery!*
Old lady: Alone she did it. She caught them alone.
Miss Kennedy: Well done, Miss Simpson.
Bank clerk: What a woman!
Miss Kennedy: Just like *Joan of Arc.*
Old lady: Boadicea, not Joan of Arc. Boadicea was British.
1st policeman: Take the stockings off their heads, Bill.
2nd policeman: I'll put the *handcuffs* on them, too.
William: Auntie, look. It's the man who was in the toy shop.
Margaret: So it is!
1st policeman: I think you deserve a reward, miss.
Bank clerk: The bank usually pays one.
Bank manager: Of course, of course.

---

bravery ['breivəri] Tapferkeit
Joan of Arc ['dʒəunəv'ɑːk] Johanna von Orleans
Boadicea [ˌbəuədi'siə] britische Königin des 1. Jahrhunderts
handcuffs Handschellen

Miss Kennedy: Miss Simpson is going to Paris. I've just given her some traveller's cheques and ...
Bank manager: Don't say another word. Miss Simpson, allow us to pay your expenses.
William: But we're going for three weeks.
Margaret: William!
Bank manager: It doesn't matter. We nearly lost thousands of pounds this morning.
1st policeman: Where's the gun?
William: It's here under this chair. But it's only a ...
Margaret: Come on, William. We are very late. Goodbye, everybody.
All: Goodbye. Have a nice trip. Thank you. Thank you.
Old lady: Farewell ... Boadicea!

At last William and Margaret get outside and begin to hurry home.

William: Auntie, did you know all the time it was the man in the toy shop?
Margaret: Of course. I *recognized* his voice. And he told me I opened my mouth too often, when I'd only spoken once.
William: Then you knew the gun wasn't a real one, too.
Margaret: I guessed it. Why?
William: Well, what about the reward for bravery? Perhaps we shouldn't take it.
Margaret: Of course we'll take it. You see, William, it isn't only a reward for bravery, it's a reward for *intelligence,* too.

to recognize ['rekəgnaiz] wiedererkennen
intelligence [in'telidʒəns] Intelligenz

Questions

1. Why do William and Margaret go to the toy shop?
2. Margaret thinks children should not play with guns. What do you *think*?
3. What do Margaret and the boy's father buy?
4. Why do William and Margaret go to the bank?
5. How much money are they going to take with them to Paris?
6. Why have the two men got stockings on their heads?
7. Why does the robber tell William to jump over the counter?
8. What does Margaret do when the robber says "On the floor, everybody"?
9. What happens when the police arrive?
10. Why did Margaret show such bravery?

The Case of the Diamond Bracelet

William and Margaret have gone into a restaurant in London for a late lunch. The restaurant is called "The Blackberry".

William: This table is free.
Margaret: But I like to sit at the window.
William: Those at the window are all taken, and you get a good view of the television from here.
Margaret: All right. Sit down, then. But I don't like television when I'm eating; it takes away my *appetite*.
William: What are *you* going to have? *I'm* hungry.
Margaret: I think I'll have fish. What about you?
William: I'm going to have a pork chop – a big one.
Margaret: But there isn't an 'r' in the month. You should only eat pork when there's an 'r' in the month.
William: And today is Monday. You should never eat fish on a Monday.
Margaret: Well, it won't hurt us to have something we shouldn't have, just once. Now, where's the waiter?
William: Auntie, have you dropped your *glove?*
Margaret: No, why?
William: Because I've got my foot on something and I think it's a glove.
Margaret: Pick it up and see.
William: Yes, it *is* a glove. Look.

diamond ['daiəmənd] Diamant
bracelet ['breislət] Armband
appetite ['æpitait] Appetit
glove [glʌv] Handschuh

Margaret: It's an old driving glove. The person who has lost that thing is not going to worry too much.
William: But it's heavy. There's something inside it.
Margaret: Hold it up and see.

William holds the glove up and a wonderful diamond bracelet falls on to the table.

Margaret: Good heavens! What a beautiful bracelet! Look at those diamonds.
William: There must be more than twenty. Are they real, do you think?
Margaret: Oh yes, they're real. Anyone can see that. It must be worth thousands.
William: The *clasp* is broken.
Margaret: That's probably why it came off and was lost.
William: But how could it slip into the glove? And anyway the glove doesn't seem to go with it.
Margaret: How do you mean?
William: It looks like a man's glove.
Margaret: Yes, you're right, it does, although it isn't *very* big.
William: The waiter's coming this way. Shall we give the bracelet to him?
Margaret: Certainly not. Quick. I'll put the bracelet on and you put the glove in your pocket. We'll decide about it later.
William: How can you put the bracelet on when the clasp is broken?
Margaret: With this little *safety-pin,* of course.

clasp Spange
safety-pin Sicherheitsnadel

At last the waiter arrives at their table and they are soon enjoying their fish and pork chop. When they are drinking their coffee they return to the subject of the bracelet.

William: Why don't you keep the bracelet? I'll give it to you.
Margaret: It isn't yours to give.
William: But I found it, didn't I?
Margaret: It doesn't belong to you just because you found it. Somebody will be very *upset* that they've lost it.
William: Shall we leave it with the manager, then?
Margaret: If we do, perhaps he'll keep it for himself, or give it to his wife. No, I'll just wear it for one day and then take it to the police station.

to upset bestürzen

William: Ah, at last they've turned the television on. I hope it's "Upstairs, downstairs".

Margaret: No, it isn't anything interesting – just police *announcements*. I prefer to watch the other people in the restaurant.

William: But, Auntie, look. There's a picture of our bracelet. You can see that the clasp is the same and that it's broken.

Margaret: Oh yes, it's the same all right. And what are they saying now?

William: That it's the famous Minster bracelet and that it was stolen last night from the house of Lady Minster here in London. Isn't that exciting?

Margaret: No, it isn't exciting at all. It's terrible. They'll think I've stolen it. Oh dear, what shall I do now? You should never pick up things that don't belong to you.

William: Push it under your dress so that nobody will see it. Quickly. The waiter's coming back. Shall we take it to the police at once? You always say we should help them.

Margaret: This time it'll be too dangerous. They'll ask me how I got it.

William: Then just throw it away when we leave the restaurant.

Margaret: Throw it away? But it's worth thousands of pounds. Nobody ever throws away diamonds. No, it's quite simple. We'll take it to Lady Minster herself.

William: Well, there's the address. They've just put it on television. The house is very near here.

Margaret: Of course. Why didn't I think of it before? Then we'll meet a member of the *aristocracy*.

William: Perhaps she'll even give us a reward.

---

announcement Ansage, Durchsage
aristocracy [ærisˈtɔkrəsi] Aristokratie

Margaret: A word of thanks from a great lady will be its own reward. Come on, William.

They pay the bill and leave the restaurant. After a short walk they arrive in a square with a garden in the middle and ring the doorbell at a large house. A *maid* looks down her nose at them but lets them in when they say they have important information about the Minster bracelet. Lady Minster, a tall woman with grey hair, gives them a cold welcome.

Lady Minster: I hope you don't write for the newspapers.
William: Oh no, we're *private detectives*.
Lady Minster: Oh dear. Really?
Margaret: William! No, Lady Minster, we just wanted to help you. We heard about the bracelet. It was on television.
Lady Minster: But I'm very upset today and anyway I don't usually see people I don't know. The police are doing all they can.
Margaret: Have they found who stole it yet?
Lady Minster: Oh no, there are thousands of criminals in London, you know. And I'll never see my bracelet again. Of course they'll have to break it into pieces. They won't be able to sell it as it is.
William: Why not?
Lady Minster: It's very famous, you see. It's a family *heirloom*. Lady Agatha Minster helped *to hide* King Charles II in a tree

---

maid (Dienst)Mädchen
private detective ['praivətdi'tektiv] Privatdetektiv
heirloom ['ɛəluːm] Erbstück
to hide verstecken

and it was given to her because of that. It's a terrible shock to
lose it like this.

Margaret: Don't worry. You haven't lost it.

Lady Minster: What do you mean?

Margaret: We've found it and brought it back. Here it is.

William: You *are* offering a big reward, aren't you?

Lady Minster takes the bracelet from Margaret and examines it. It is clear she is very excited but she is making a great effort to keep calm. She looks round the room as if she is frightened, then she rings the bell loudly and the maid comes in.

Lady Minster: Oh, Mary, ask Mr Best to come here a moment, please. You don't mind if I show this to a friend, do you?

Margaret: Not at all.

Maid: He was just coming to see you himself, My Lady. Here he is.

Lady Minster: Ah, there you are, Inspector Best. Arrest these two *confidence tricksters* at once. They are *pretending* this *replica* is the Minster bracelet and are asking for a big reward.

Margaret: Well, I have never been so insulted ...

William: ... when we were trying to help.

Inspector: Don't move, you two. I have men all over the house. May I look at the bracelet? Hm! Very interesting. Did you know there was such a perfect replica, My Lady?

Lady Minster: Er ... of course. It was made for me. It's too dangerous to wear the real thing these days, you know.

---

confidence trickster ['kɔnfidəns'trikstə] Hochstapler
to pretend vorgeben, -täuschen
replica ['replikə] Kopie

Inspector: You didn't tell me they had stolen two bracelets. And you kept the replica in your jewel case with the real one?

Lady Minster: That's right.

Margaret: What are you doing with those handcuffs?

Inspector: I'm going to put them on you – unless you explain yourself. Where did you get this bracelet?

Margaret: It was under our table in a restaurant near here.

William: I put my foot on it. That's how we found it.

Margaret: It's a very good restaurant. Only the best people go there. It's called "The Blackberry".

Lady Minster: What a silly story! Nobody's going to believe that. It's clear that they stole both and are going to sell the real one.

Inspector: The replica is certainly a very good one. May I see the photo of the real one again?

Lady Minster: Of course, Inspector. I have it in my bag.

Lady Minster takes the photo out of her bag and gives it to Inspector Best. At the same time a glove falls out of the bag on to the floor. William, like a perfect gentleman, rushes to pick it up.

William: You've dropped your glove, My Lady.

Lady Minster: Give it to me. It's only one of my driving gloves.

William: But it's just like the one in the restaurant. They make a pair.

Lady Minster: Give it to me, boy.

Margaret: Be quick, William. And give Lady Minster the other one, too, the one you found in the restaurant with the bracelet in it.

Inspector: The bracelet was in a glove, was it? May I see both gloves, please.

27

William gives Inspector Best the glove Lady Minster has dropped and the one he put in his pocket in the restaurant.

Inspector: They certainly make a pair. Did you know this glove was missing, My Lady?
Lady Minster: Oh yes, I've been looking everywhere for it.
Inspector: And as the bracelet was in the glove, the person who stole the bracelet ...
Lady Minster: Bracelets.
Inspector: ... Excuse me, the bracelets, ... probably stole the glove, too.
Lady Minster: That's right. I never thought of that. You *are* clever, Inspector. Of course I've always thought the British police were wonderful.

There is a knock at the door and the maid comes in.

Maid: The gentleman from the *insurance company*, My Lady.
Lady Minster: Ask him to wait. I'm very busy at the moment.
Inspector: May I ask him a few questions, Lady Minster?
Lady Minster: I really haven't much time. I don't know ...
Inspector: It won't take a minute.
Lady Minster: Oh, very well. Ask Mr Potter to come in, Mary. But I don't know how *he* can help.
Inspector: Good afternoon, Mr Potter. I'm Inspector Best of Scotland Yard. Please look carefully at this bracelet. Is it the one you *insured* for Lady Minster?

---

insurance [inˈʃuərəns] Versicherung
company Gesellschaft
to insure versichern

Potter: Certainly. I'm so glad it has been found. Yes, yes. This is the Minster bracelet all right.

Inspector: Why are you so sure?

Potter: For two *reasons*. The third diamond from the right has a little *flaw* in it.

Inspector: So it has!

Potter: And the clasp is broken.

Margaret: Thank heavens! So it isn't a replica.

Potter: Oh no. This is the original Charles II clasp and anyway there *is* no replica.

Inspector: How do you know that?

Potter: It was one of the *conditions* of the insurance. No replica must be made. How did you get the bracelet back?

Inspector: This lady found it under her table in "The Blackberry".

Potter: The company *will* be glad.

Margaret: But Lady Minster doesn't look very happy.

Lady Minster: I'm not feeling very well. I must go to my room for a moment. I am too upset to ...

Inspector: Stay where you are. Lady Minster, I arrest you in the name of the *law*.

Lady Minster: Oh dear ...

William: Quick, she's fainted.

Margaret: Open the window, somebody.

Inspector: She'll be all right in a moment. Ring the bell for the maid.

---

reason Grund
flaw [flɔ:] Fehler
condition Bedingung
law Gesetz

The maid comes in and helps Lady Minster.

Margaret: But I don't understand. Why have you arrested her?
William: Who stole the bracelet?
Inspector: Nobody stole it. She herself threw it away.
Potter: Threw away a diamond bracelet insured for £12,000? That can't be true.
Inspector: Oh yes, Mr Potter. You see, since her husband died Lady Minster has spent too much money, I'm afraid, and the only way to pay her *debts* was to sell the Minster bracelet. She had nothing else left. But she couldn't sell it because it's a family heirloom and was only hers while she lived. After she died it had to go to her son's wife, and Lady Minster hates her

debts [dets] Schulden

son's wife. So she pretended it had been stolen in order to get the insurance. Of course she didn't offer a reward because she didn't *want* to get the bracelet back. And she *expected* that the finder would keep such a wonderful thing for himself, or sell it.

William: It's just like a detective story. How did you find the truth, Inspector?

Inspector: *You* helped me to find the truth, you and this lady here. Not only because you brought the bracelet but because you brought the glove. When I saw the glove, I knew the answer.

Margaret: Poor woman. Will she go to *prison?*

Potter: Well, it's *fraud,* you know, and fraud against *my* company.

William: But as she didn't manage to get the insurance, perhaps it won't be so bad for her.

Inspector: Let's hope not. And now perhaps you two will come to Scotland Yard with Mr Potter and myself.

Margaret: In handcuffs, Inspector?

Inspector: Good heavens, no! As important guests. I want to introduce two *professional* detectives to some of the amateurs!

---

to expect erwarten
prison ['prizn] Gefängnis
fraud [frɔːd] Betrug
professional [prəˈfeʃənəl] beruflich, Berufs...

Questions

1. What do William and Margaret want to eat at "The Blackberry" restaurant?
2. What is wrong with the bracelet?
3. What do William and Margaret see on television?
4. What do they decide to do with the bracelet?
5. What does Lady Minster tell them about the history of the bracelet?
6. What does Lady Minster tell the inspector about William and Margaret?
7. What do you know about the glove that falls out of Lady Minster's bag?
8. How does Mr Potter know that the bracelet is not a replica?
9. Why does Lady Minster faint?
10. Why did Lady Minster pretend that the bracelet had been stolen?